Wedding Songs

FOR UKULELE

T0066174

ISBN 978-1-4950-6100-4

HAL•LEONARD®
CORPORATION

7777 W. BLUEMOUND RD. P.O. BOX 13819 MILWAUKEE, WI 53213

Visit Hal Leonard Online at
www.halleonard.com

All of Me

Words and Music by John Stephens and Toby Gad

1. What would I do with-out your smart
2. How man-y times do I have to tell

mouth draw-in' me in and you kick-in' me out?
you? E - ven when you're cry-ing, you're beau-ti-ful, too.

You've got my head spin-nin', no kid-din'. I
The world is beat-ing you down. I'm a-

can't pin you down. What's go-in'
round through ev-er-y mood. You're my

on in that beau-ti-ful mind? I'm on your
down-fall, you're my muse, my worst dis-trac-

ning. 'Cause I give you all _____ of me, __

____ and you give me all _____

To Coda ⊕ | 1.

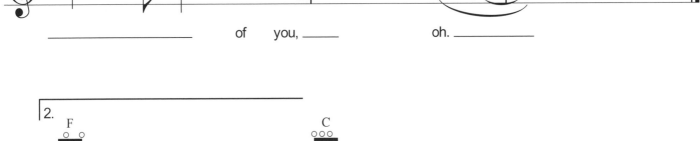

_____ of you, ____ oh. _____

| 2.

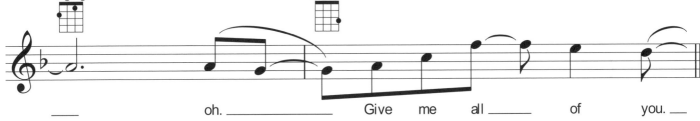

____ oh. _____ Give me all ____ of you. ____

Bridge

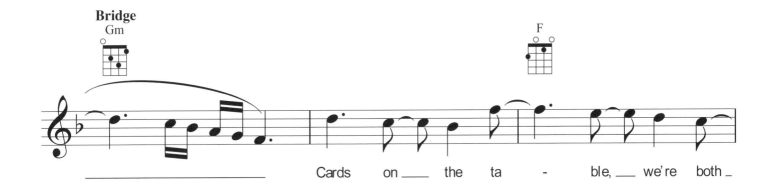

_____ Cards on ____ the ta - ble, ____ we're both ____

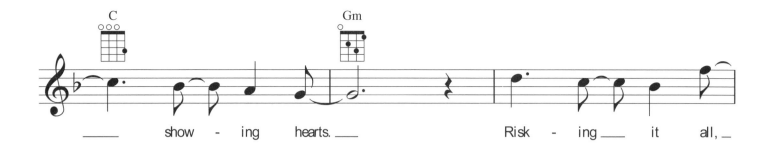

show - ing hearts. ____ Risk - ing ____ it all, ____

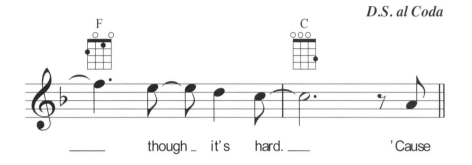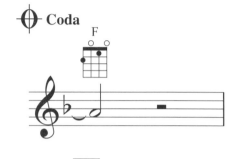

D.S. al Coda ⊕ **Coda**

though _ it's hard. ____ 'Cause ____

Outro

I give you all _____ of me, _

and you give me all _____

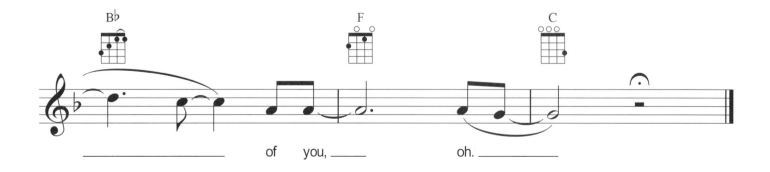

_____ of you, ____ oh. _____

Can't Help Falling in Love

from the Paramount Picture BLUE HAWAII
Words and Music by George David Weiss, Hugo Peretti and Luigi Creatore

At Last

Lyric by Mack Gordon
Music by Harry Warren

Better Together

Words and Music by Jack Johnson

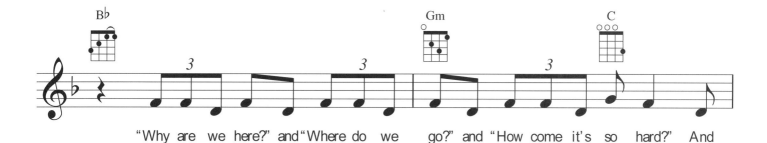

"Why are we here?" and "Where do we go?" and "How come it's so hard?" And

it's not al - ways eas - y and some - times life can be de - ceiv - ing.

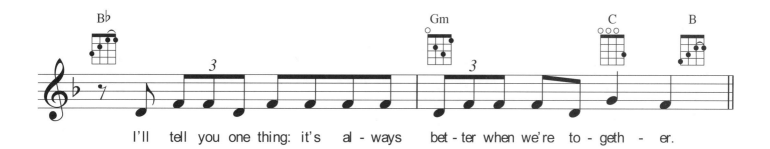

I'll tell you one thing: it's al - ways bet - ter when we're to - geth - er.

𝄋 Chorus

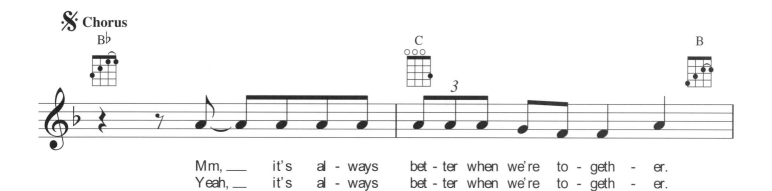

Mm, ___ it's al - ways bet - ter when we're to - geth - er.
Yeah, ___ it's al - ways bet - ter when we're to - geth - er.

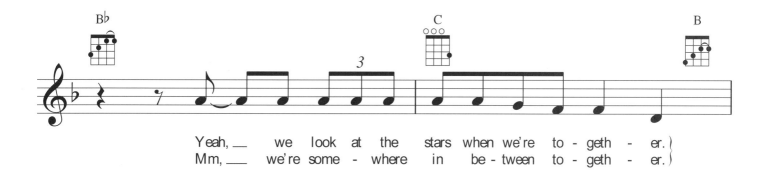

Yeah, ___ we look at the stars when we're to - geth - er.
Mm, ___ we're some - where in be - tween to - geth - er.

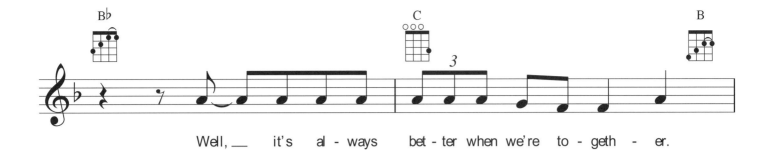

Well, __ it's al - ways bet - ter when we're to - geth - er.

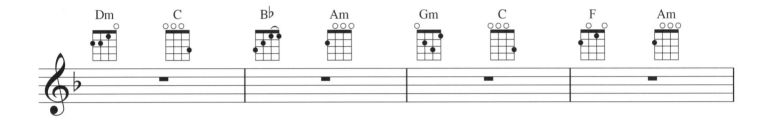

Yeah, __ it's al - ways bet - ter when we're to - geth - er. _____

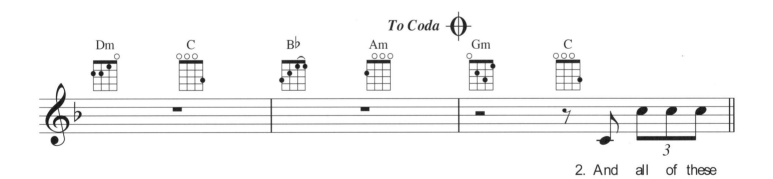

To Coda ⊕

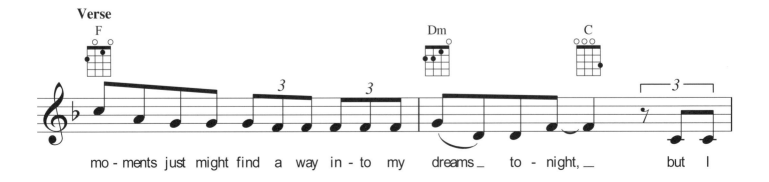

2. And all of these

Verse

mo - ments just might find a way in - to my dreams __ to - night, __ but I

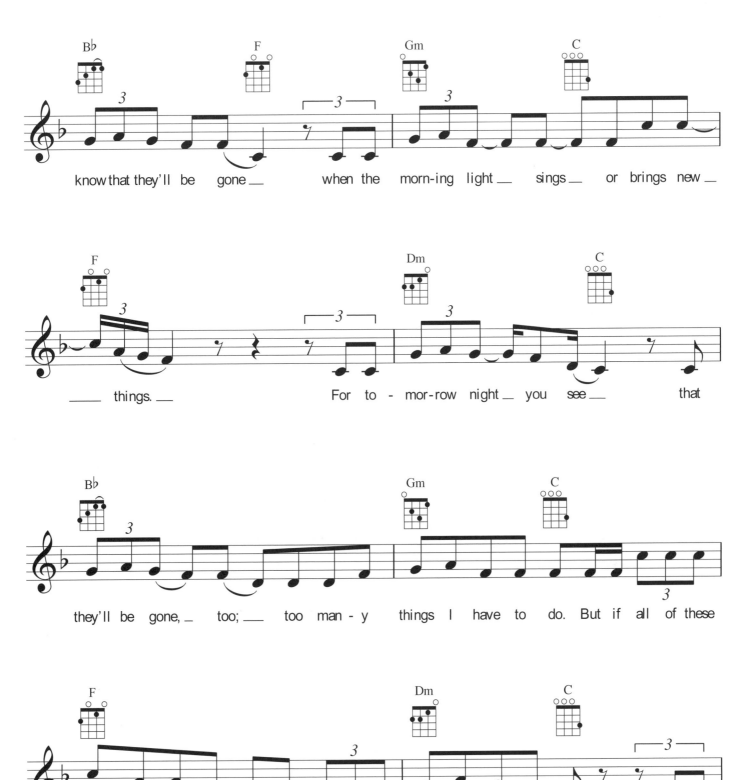

know that they'll be   gone __   when the   morn-ing light __   sings __   or brings new __

___ things. __   For to - mor-row night __   you   see __   that

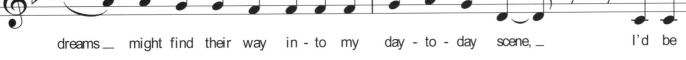

they'll be gone, __   too; __   too man - y   things I   have to   do. But if   all of these

dreams __   might find their   way in - to my   day - to - day   scene, __   I'd be

un - der the im - pres - sion   I was   some-where in be - tween __   with on - ly

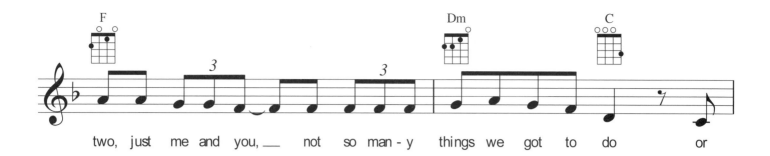

two, just me and you, ___ not so man-y things we got to do or

D.S. al Coda

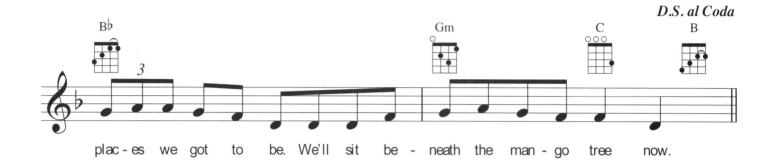

plac-es we got to be. We'll sit be - neath the man-go tree now.

Coda

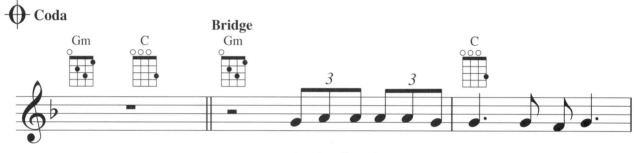
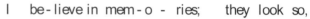

Bridge

I be-lieve in mem-o - ries; they look so,

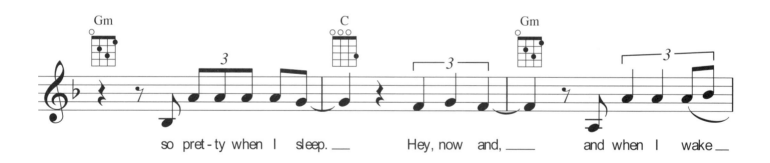

so pret-ty when I sleep. ___ Hey, now and, ___ and when I wake ___

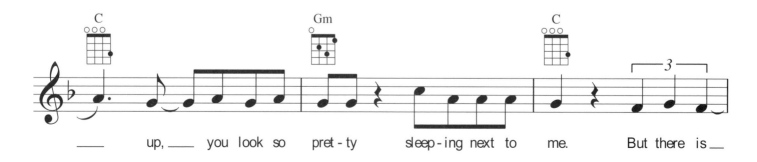

___ up, ___ you look so pret-ty sleep-ing next to me. But there is ___

not e - nough time. _____ And there is no, ___

___ no song I could sing. ___ And there is no ___

___ com - bi - na - tion of words ___ I could say, ___ but I will

Outro

still tell you one thing: ___ We're bet - ter to - geth - er. _____

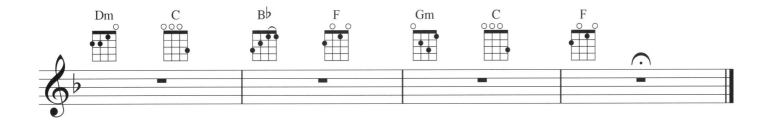

Everything

Words and Music by Amy Foster-Gillies, Michael Bublé and Alan Chang

smile at me, you know ex - act - ly what you do. Ba - by, don't
get to kiss you, ba - by, just be - cause I can. What - ev - er

pre - tend that you don't know it's true, 'cause you can
comes our way, oh, we'll see it through. And you know

see it when I look at you. And in _____ this cra -
_____ that's what our love can do.

Chorus

- zy _____ life, _____ and through these cra - zy times, _

_____ it's you, _ it's you. You make me sing. ___ You're ev -'ry line, _

19

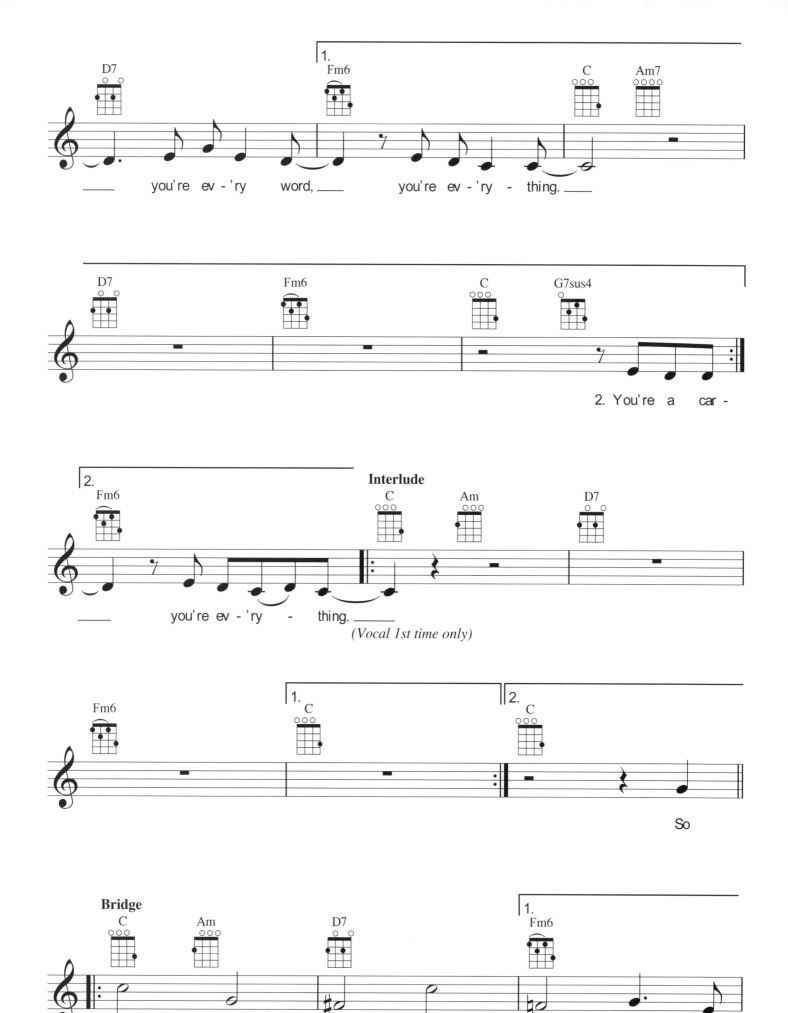

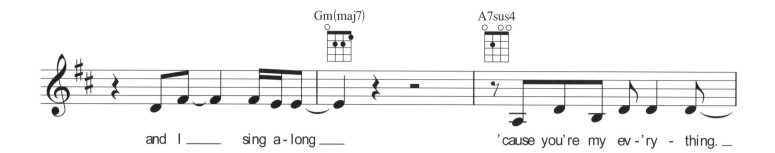

and I _____ sing a-long _____ 'cause you're my ev-'ry - thing. __

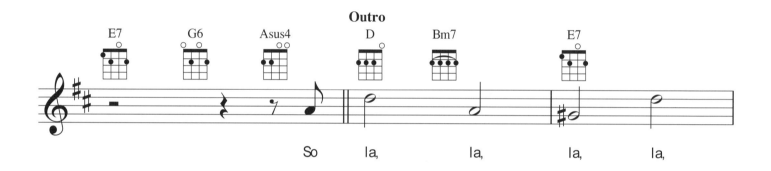

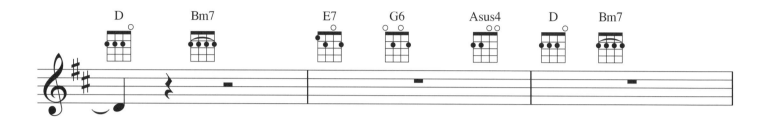

Outro

So la, la, la, la,

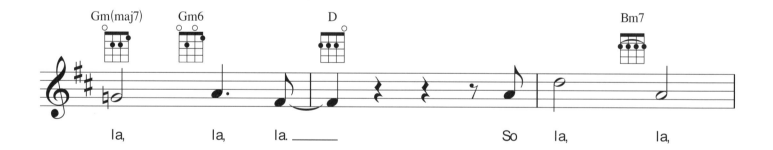

la, la, la. _____ So la, la,

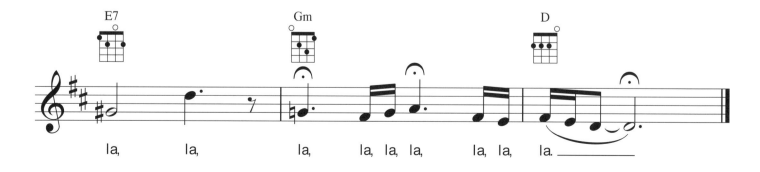

la, la, la, la, la, la, la, la. _____

I Will

Words and Music by John Lennon and Paul McCartney

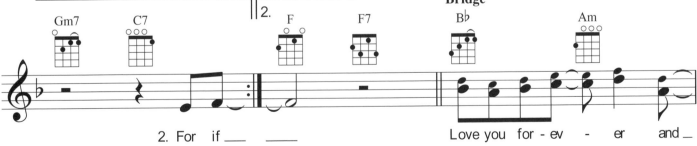

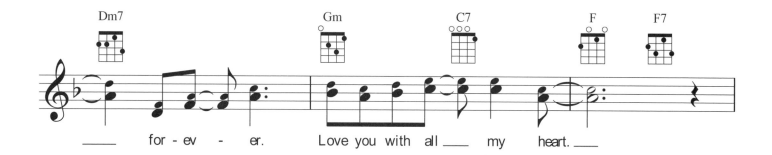

_____ for - ev - er. Love you with all ___ my heart. ___

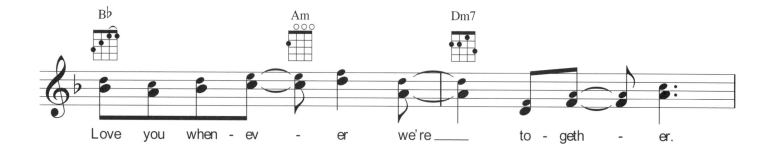

Love you when - ev - er we're _____ to - geth - er.

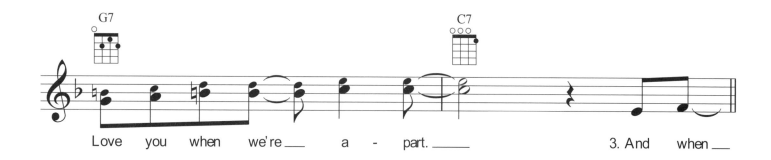

Love you when we're ___ a - part. _____ 3. And when ___

Verse

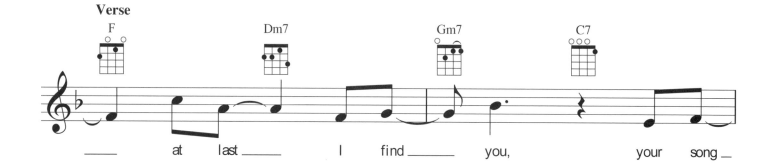

_____ at last _____ I find _____ you, your song ___

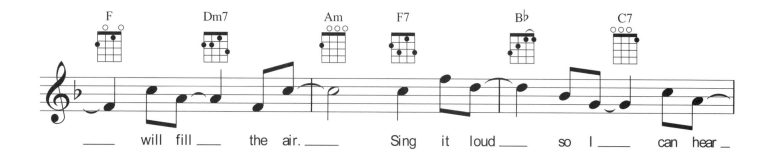

_____ will fill ___ the air. _____ Sing it loud ___ so I ___ can hear _

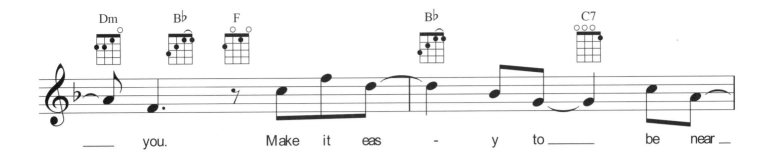

you. Make it eas - y to _____ be near _____

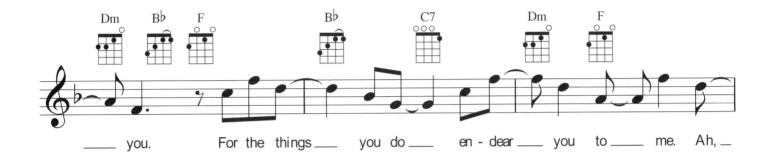

you. For the things _____ you do _____ en - dear _____ you to _____ me. Ah, _____

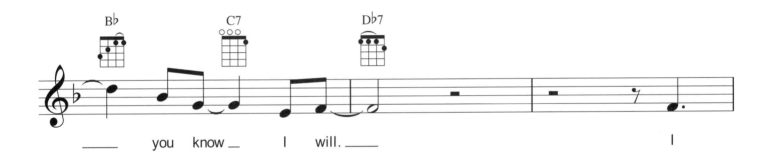

_____ you know _____ I will. _____   I

Outro

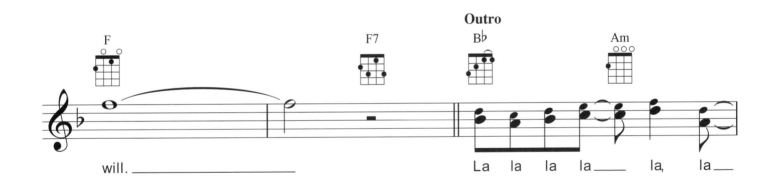

will. _____   La la la la _____ la, la _____

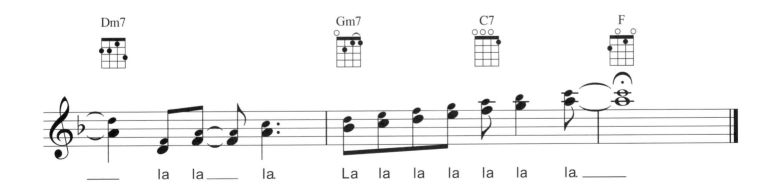

_____ la la _____ la.   La la la la la la la. _____

Grow Old with Me

Words and Music by John Lennon

Additional Lyrics

2. Grow old along with me,
   Two branches of one tree.
   Face the setting sun
   When the day is done.
   God bless our love,
   God bless our love.

3. Grow old along with me,
   Whatever fate decrees.
   We will see it through,
   For our love is true.
   God bless our love,
   God bless our love.

The Hawaiian Wedding Song
(Ke Kali Nei Au)

English Lyrics by Al Hoffman and Dick Manning
Hawaiian Lyrics and Music by Charles E. King

I'm Yours

Words and Music by Jason Mraz

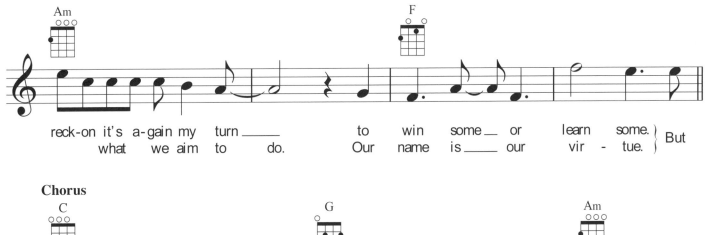

reck-on it's a-gain my turn _____ to win some _ or learn some. } But
what we aim to do. Our name is _____ our vir - tue. }

Chorus

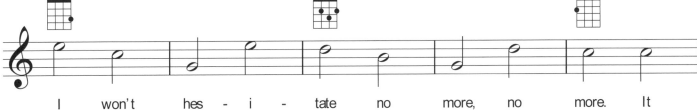

I won't hes - i - tate no more, no more. It

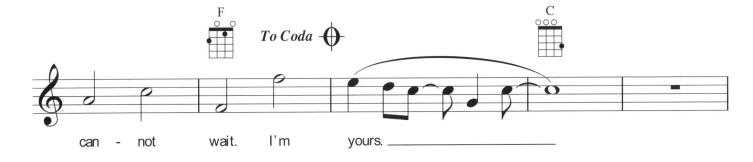

To Coda ⊕

can - not wait. I'm yours. _____

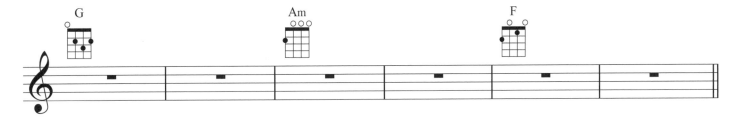

Bridge

2. Well, o - pen up your mind and see _ like me. _ O - pen up your

plans and, damn, _ you're free. _ Look in - to your heart and you'll _ find

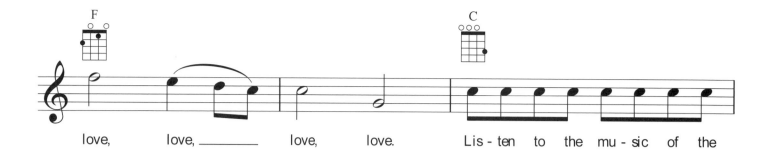

love, love, _____ love, love. Lis - ten to the mu - sic of the

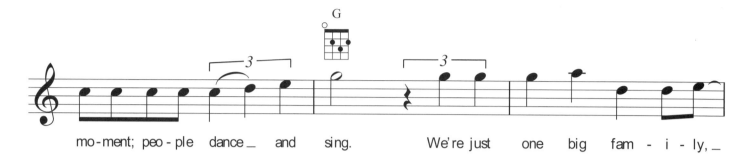

mo - ment; peo - ple dance _ and sing. We're just one big fam - i - ly, _

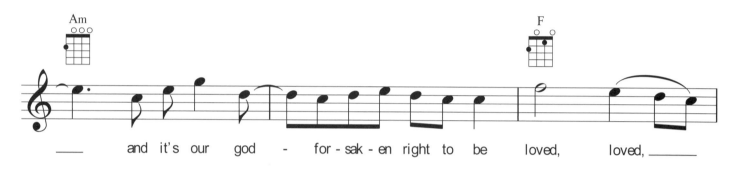

_ and it's our god - for - sak - en right to be loved, loved, _____

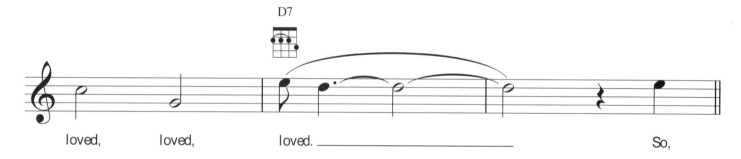

loved, loved, loved. _____ So,

Chorus

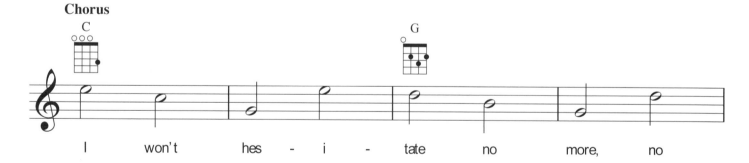

I won't hes - i - tate no more, no

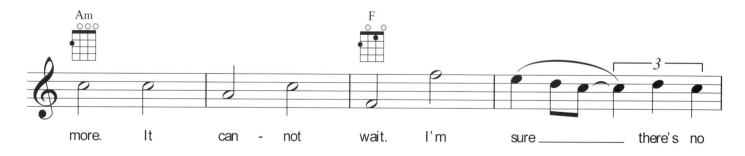

more. It can - not wait. I'm sure _____ there's no

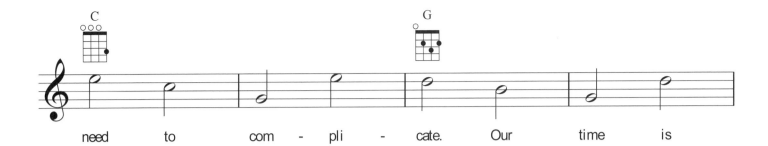

need   to   com - pli - cate.   Our   time   is

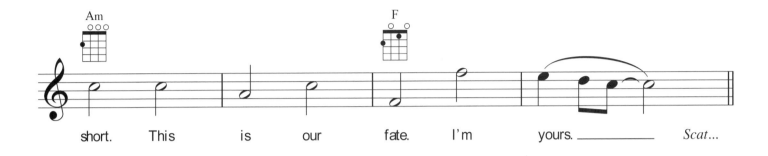

short.   This   is   our   fate.   I'm   yours. _____   *Scat...*

Interlude

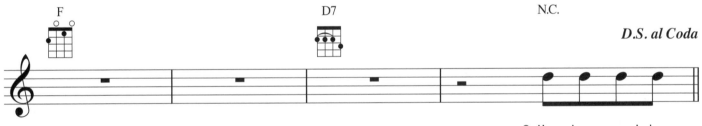

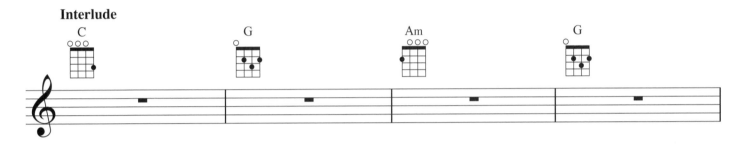

D.S. al Coda

3. I've been spend-ing

Coda   **Bridge/Chorus**

yours. _____

(I   won't   hes - i -

Well, o - pen up your   mind   and see   like

me.   O - pen up your   plans   and, damn, __ you're   free.   Look in - to your

tate   no   more,   no   more.   It

heart and you'll _ find that the sky is yours. _____ So,
can - not wait the sky I'm sure. _____ No

please don't, please don't, please don't... There's no need __ to com - pli -
need to com - pli - cate. Our

cate 'cause our time is short. _ This is, this is, this is our
time is short. This is our

fate. I'm yours. _____ *Scat...*
fate. I'm yours.) _____

Outro

Repeat and fade

The Way I Am

Words and Music by Ingrid Michaelson

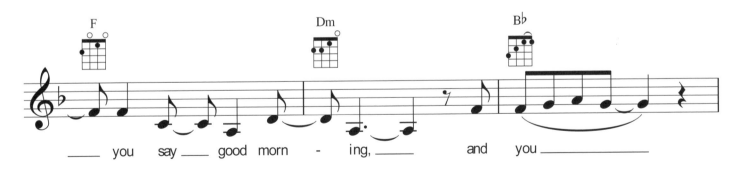

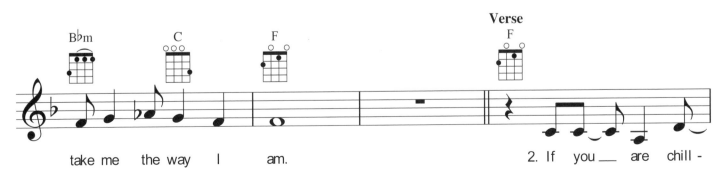

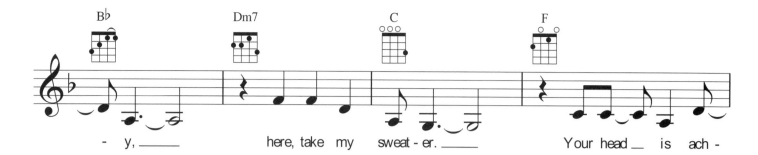

- y, _____ here, take my sweat-er. _____ Your head _____ is ach -

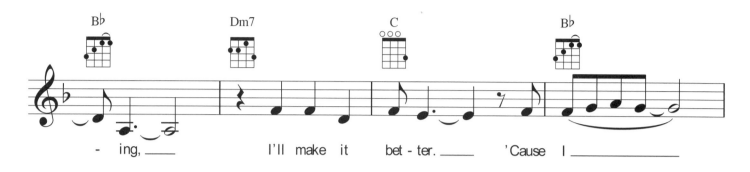

- ing, _____ I'll make it bet-ter. _____ 'Cause I _____

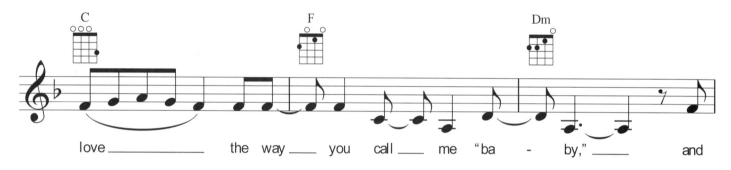

love _____ the way _____ you call _____ me "ba - by," _____ and

you _____ take me the way I am.

Verse

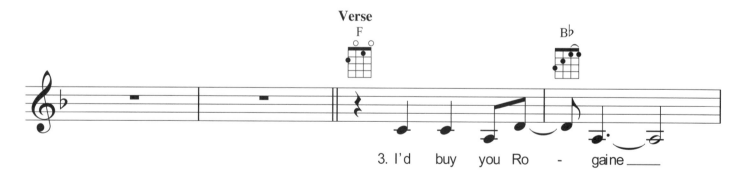

3. I'd buy you Ro - gaine _____

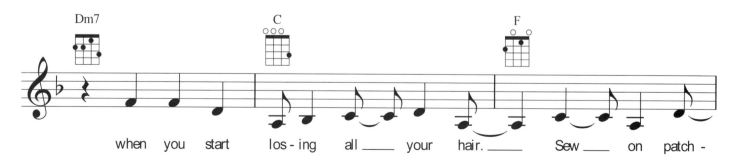

when you start los-ing all _____ your hair. _____ Sew _____ on patch -

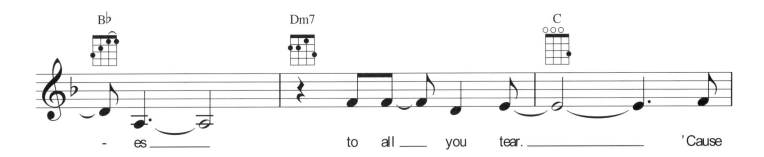

-es _____ to all ___ you tear. _____ 'Cause

I _____ love _ you more _ than I _____ could ev – er prom –

– ise, _____ and you _____ take me the way I

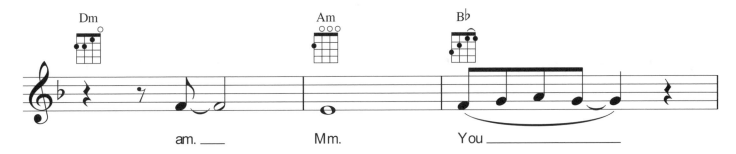

am. ___ Mm. You _____

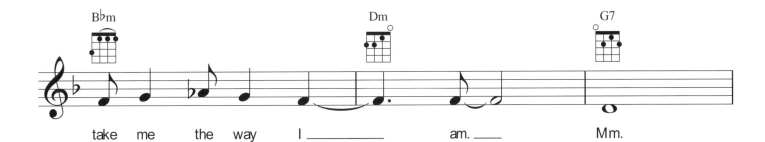

take me the way I _____ am. ___ Mm.

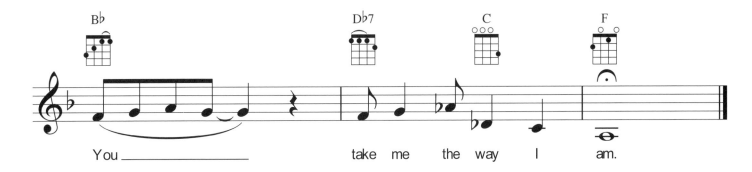

You _____ take me the way I am.

In My Life

Words and Music by John Lennon and Paul McCartney

dead __ and __ some __ are __ liv - ing;   in my _____ life I've

know I'll of - ten stop and think a - bout them;   in my _____ life I

To Coda Interlude

loved them all. __
love you more. __

(Instrumental)

1.

2.   ***D.S. al Coda***
        (Lyric 2)

Though I

Coda
Outro

(Instrumental)   In my _____ life I

N.C.

love you more.
(Instrumental)

Just the Way You Are

Words and Music by Billy Joel

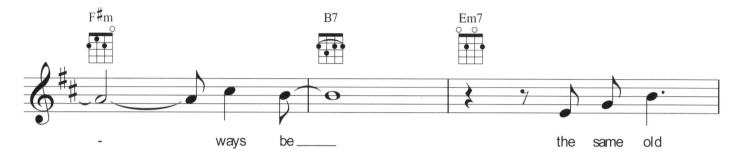

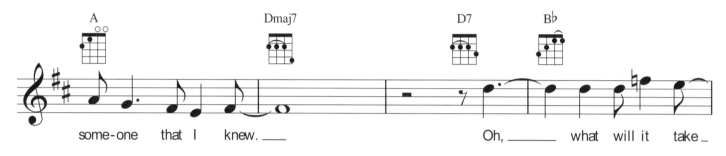

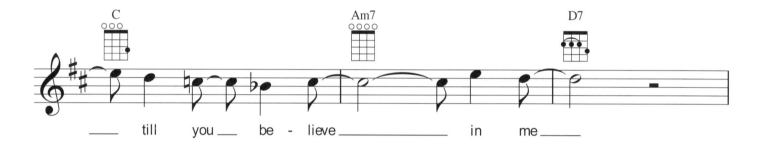

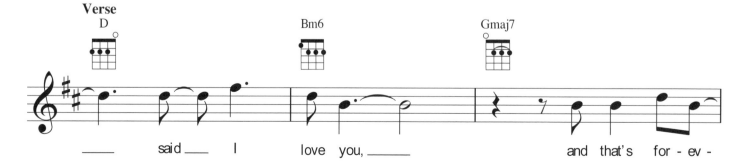

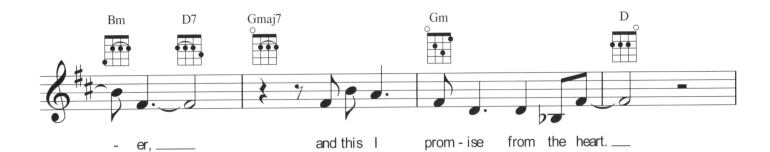

- er, _____ and this I prom - ise from the heart. __

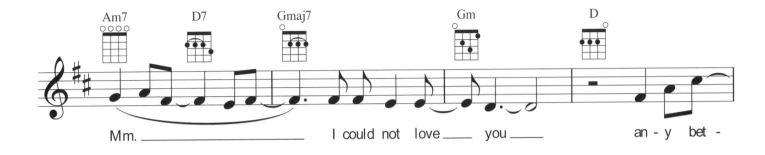

Mm. _____ I could not love _____ you _____ an - y bet -

- ter; I love _ you just _____ the way _____ you are. __

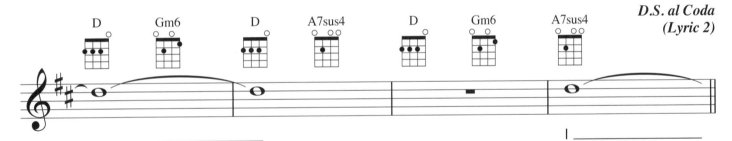

D.S. al Coda
(Lyric 2)

I _____

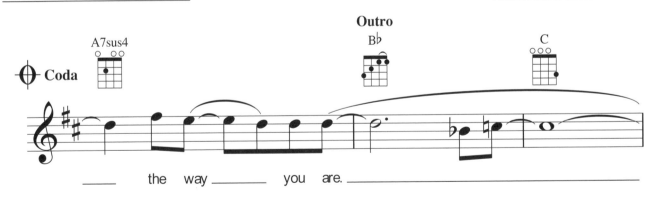

Outro

_____ the way _____ you are. _____

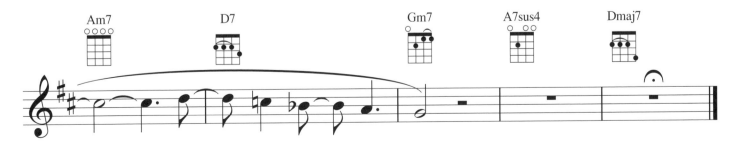

Marry Me

Words and Music by David Katz, Pat Monahan and Sam Hollander

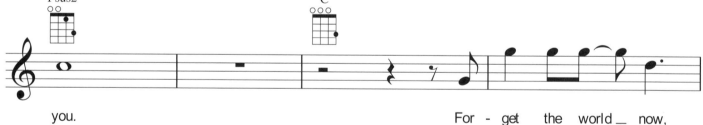

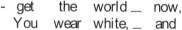

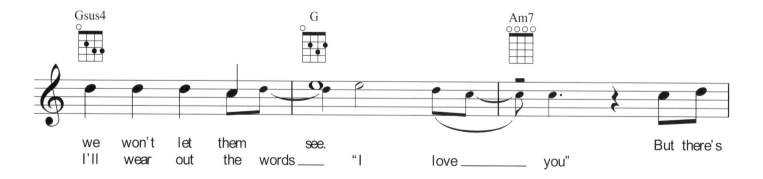

1. For - ev - er could nev - er be long e - nough __ for me __
2. To - geth - er can nev - er be close e - nough __ for me __

___ to feel like I've had long e - nough __ with
___ to feel like I am close e - nough __ to

you.
you.

For - get the world __ now,
You wear white, __ and

we won't let them see.
I'll wear out the words ___ "I love _____ you"

But there's

one thing left to do: _____   Now
and "you're beau-ti-ful." _   Now

that the weight _ has lift - ed, ___   and
that the wait ___ is o - ver ___

love has sure - ly _____ shift - ed my way, _
love has fi - n'lly _____ showed ___ her my way, _

mar - ry me,

to - day ___ and ev - 'ry _____ day. _

Mar - ry me.

If I ev - er get ___ the nerve ___ to say ___ "hel - lo" ___

___ in this ___ ca - fé, ___ say you will, ___

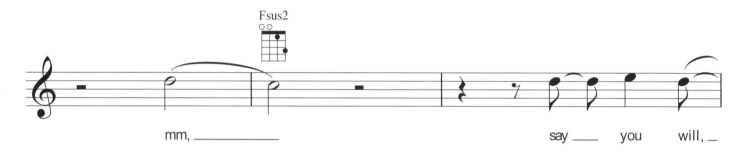

mm, ___ say ___ you will, ___

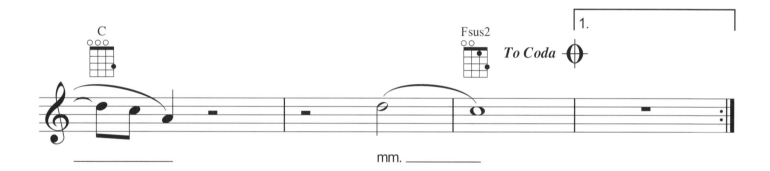

1.

To Coda ⊕

___ mm. ___

2. **Bridge**

Prom - ise me you'll al -

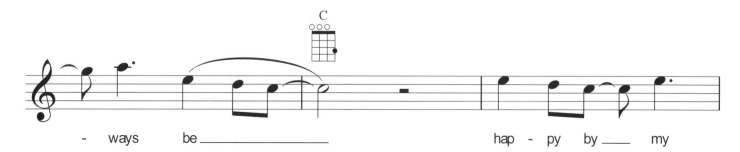

- ways be ___ hap - py by ___ my

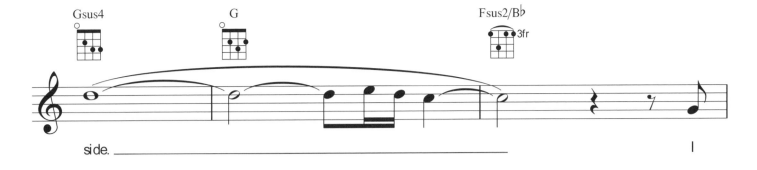

side. _____ I

prom - ise   to   sing ____ to you _____

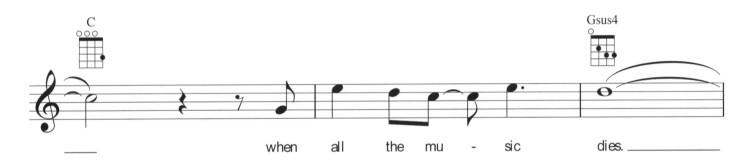

____   when all   the   mu - sic   dies. _____

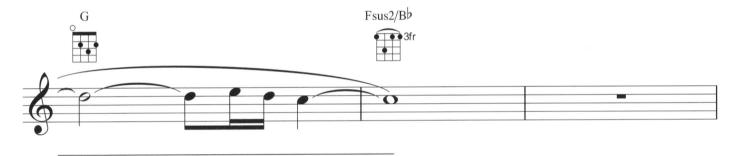

_____

D.S. al Coda

And

Coda

Mar - ry

me,   mm. _____

Thinking Out Loud

Words and Music by Ed Sheeran and Amy Wadge

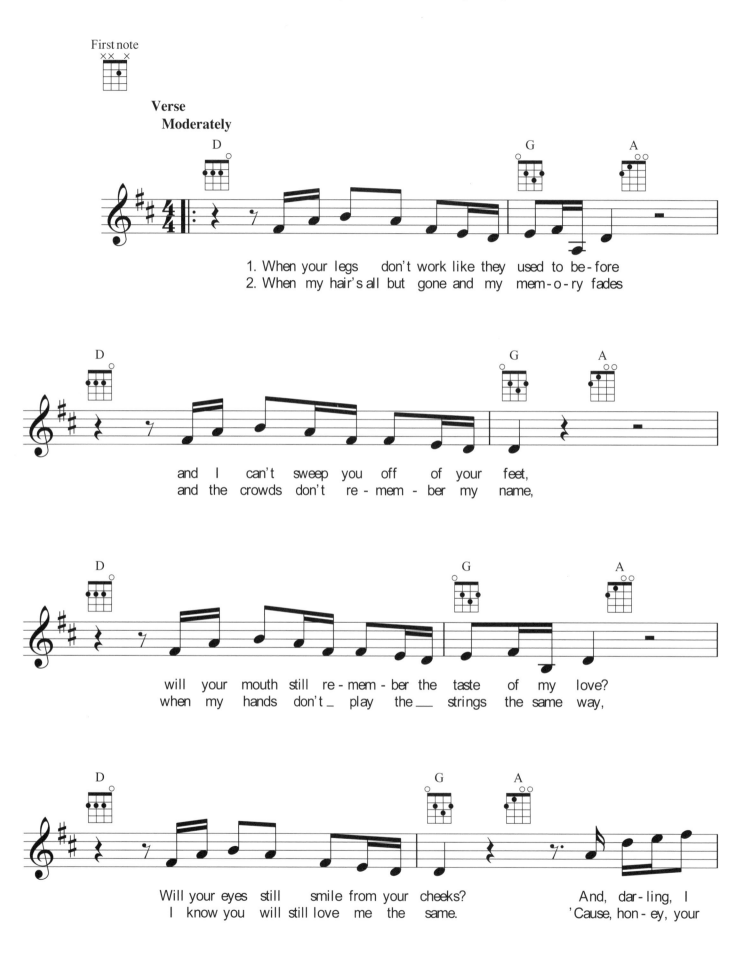

1. When your legs   don't work like they used to be-fore
2. When my hair's all but gone and my mem-o-ry fades

and I can't sweep you off of your feet,
and the crowds don't re-mem-ber my name,

will your mouth still re-mem-ber the taste of my love?
when my hands don't_ play the __ strings the same way,

Will your eyes still   smile from your cheeks?   And, dar-ling, I
I know you will still love me the   same.   'Cause, hon-ey, your

will ___ be lov-ing you   till ___ we're sev-en-ty. ___
soul ___ could nev-er grow   old; ___ it's ev-er-green. ___

___
___

And, ba-by, my
And, ba-by, your

heart ___ could still feel as   hard ___ at twen-ty-three. ___
smile's ___ for-ev-er in   my mind ___ and mem-o-ry. ___

_____
_____

And I'm think-ing 'bout   how ___
And I'm think-ing 'bout   how ___

Pre-Chorus

peo-ple fall in love in mys-te - ri-ous ways, ___
peo-ple fall in love in mys-te - ri-ous ways, ___   and

may-be just the touch of a hand. ___
may-be it's all part of a plan. ___   Well,
Well,

me, I fall in love with you ev - 'ry sin - gle day, _____ and
I'll just keep on mak - ing the same _____ mis - takes, _____

I just wan - na tell you I am. _____ So, hon - ey, now, _____
hop - ing that you'll un - der - stand _____ that, ba - by, now... _____

𝄋 Chorus

_____ take me in - to your lov - ing arms. ___

___ Kiss me un - der the light of a

thou - sand stars. _____ Place your head on my beat - ing heart. ___

___ I'm think - ing out _____ loud; _____ may - be

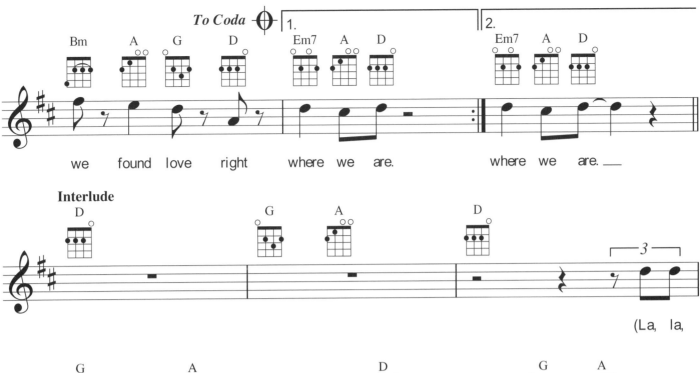

we found love right where we are.   where we are. ___

Interlude

(La, la,

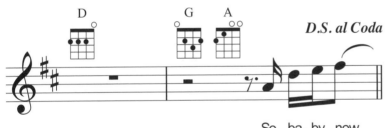

la, la, la, la, la, la, la, la, la, la, la.)

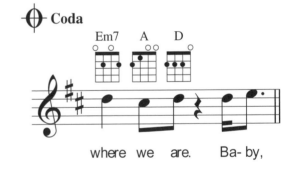

So, ba-by, now, ___   where we are. Ba-by,

Outro

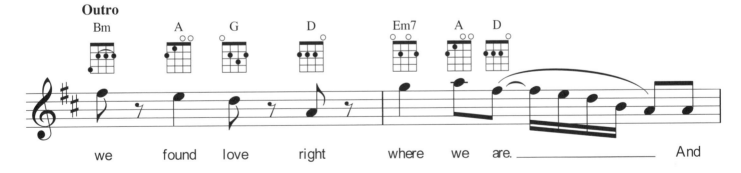

we found love right where we are. _____ And

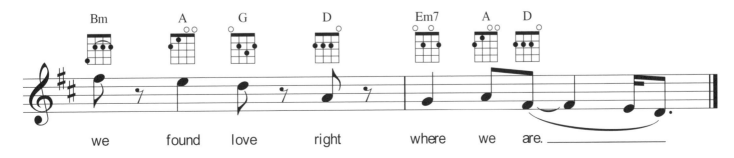

we found love right where we are. ___

A Thousand Years

from the Summit Entertainment film THE TWILIGHT SAGA: BREAKING DAWN – PART 1
Words and Music by David Hodges and Christina Perri

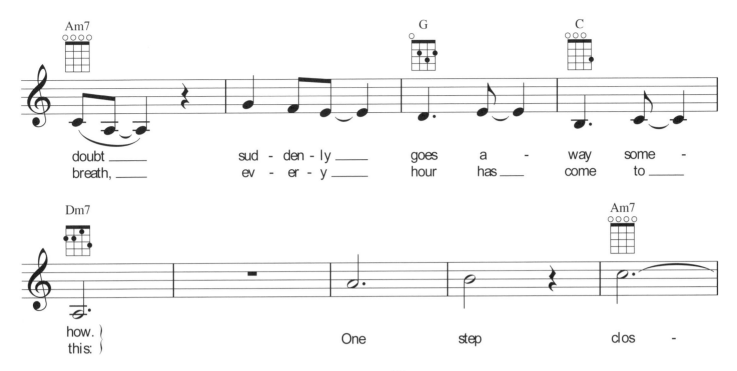

doubt _____ sud - den - ly _____ goes a - way some -
breath, _____ ev - er - y _____ hour has _____ come to _____

how. }
this: }

One step clos -

𝄋 Chorus 1

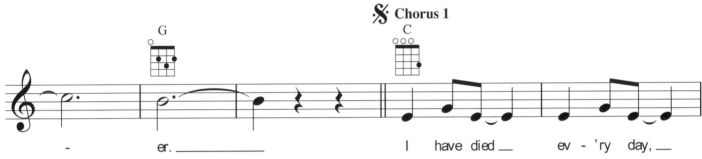

- er. _____ I have died _____ ev - 'ry day, _____

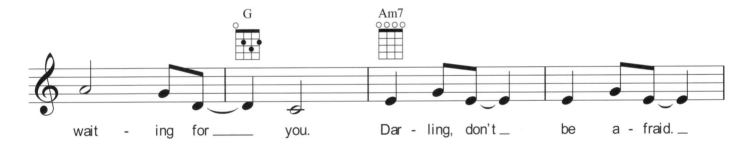

wait - ing for _____ you. Dar - ling, don't _____ be a - fraid. _____

I have loved _____ you for a thou - sand years, _____ I'll

1.

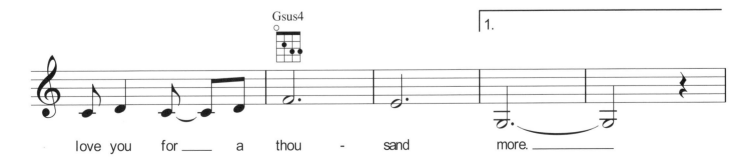

love you for _____ a thou - sand more. _____

Chorus 2

more.

And all a-long _ I be-lieved _ I would find _ you.

Time has brought _ your heart to me; _ I have loved _ you for a

thou - sand years, _ I'll love you for _ a

To Coda ⊕

Interlude

thou - sand more. _

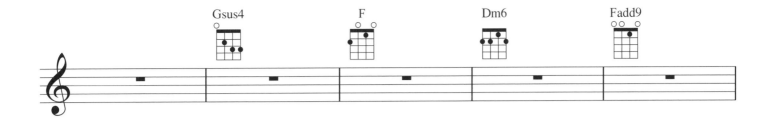

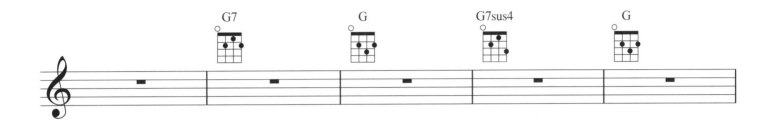

Pre-Chorus

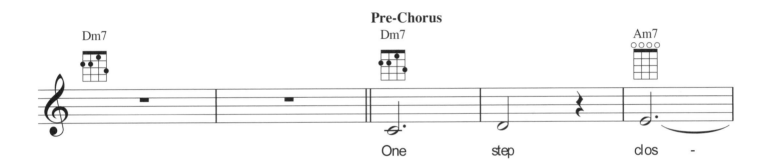

One step clos -

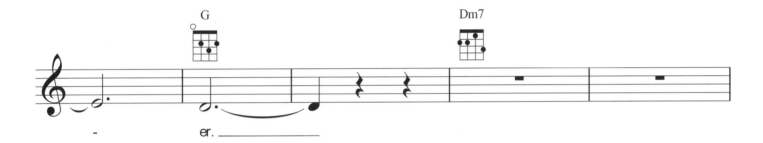

- er.

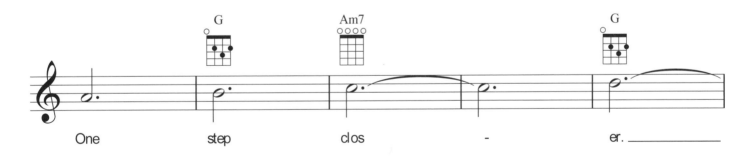

One step clos - er.

D.S. al Coda
(take 2nd ending)

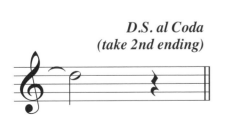

Coda

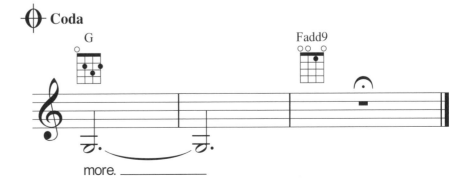

more.

Till There Was You

from Meredith Willson's THE MUSIC MAN
By Meredith Willson

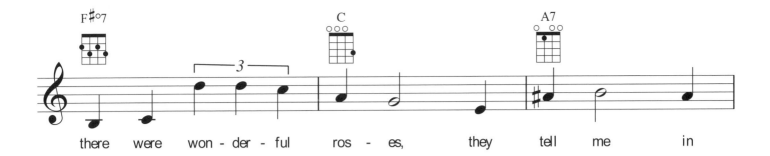

there were won - der - ful ros - es, they tell me in

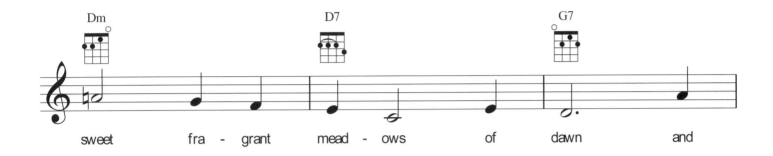

sweet fra - grant mead - ows of dawn and

Outro-Verse

dew. There was love all a - round, but I

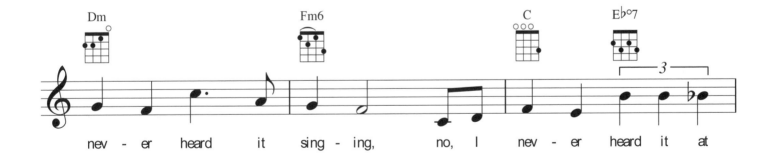

nev - er heard it sing - ing, no, I nev - er heard it at

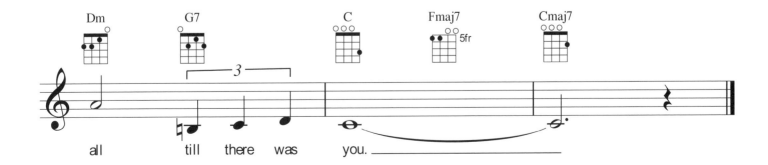

all till there was you.

The Way You Look Tonight

Words by Dorothy Fields
Music by Jerome Kern

part, _____ and that laugh that wrin - kles your nose _

___ touch - es my fool - ish heart. _____

Outro-Verse

Love - ly, nev - er, nev - er change, keep that breath - less

charm. Won't you please ar - range it 'cause I love you,

just the way you look to - night. Mm, _ mm, _ mm, _

mm, _ just the way you look to - night. _____

Wedding Song
(There Is Love)

Words and Music by Paul Stookey

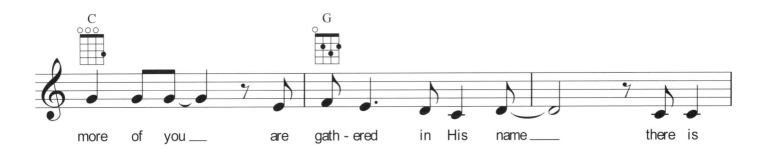

more of you ___ are gath-ered in His name ___ there is

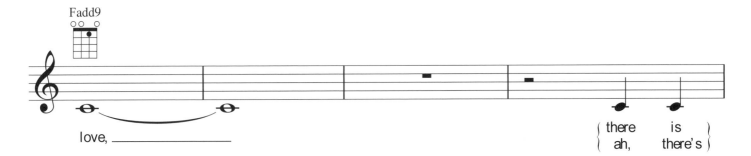

love, ___

there is
ah, there's

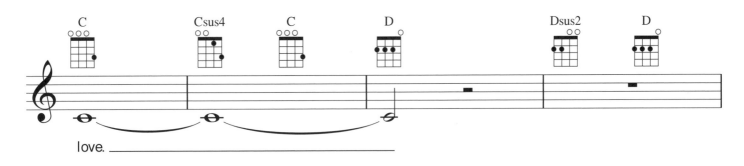

love. ___

To Coda

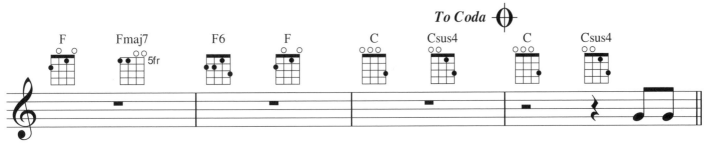

2. Well, a

Verse

man shall leave his moth-er, and a wom-an leave ___ her home, ___

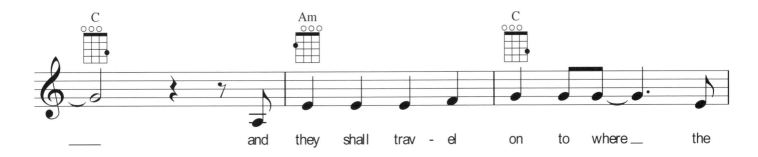

___ and they shall trav-el on to where ___ the

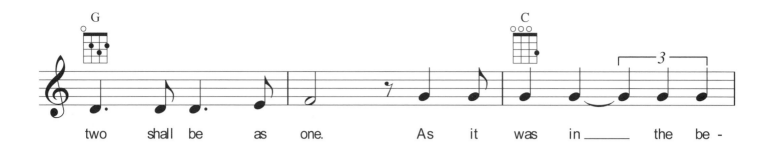

two   shall   be   as   one.   As   it   was   in _____ the   be -

gin - ning,   is   now   un - til   the   end.

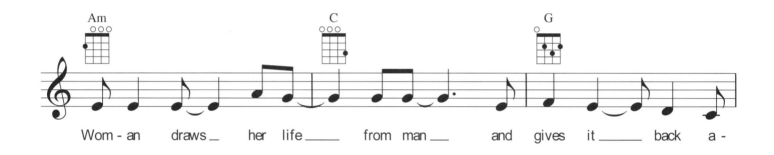

Wom - an   draws _ her   life _____ from   man _ and   gives   it _____ back   a -

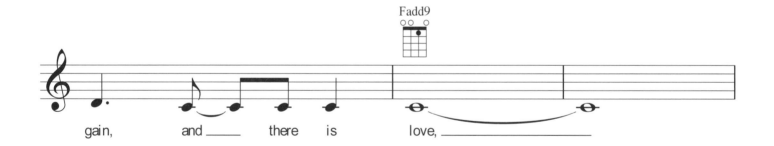

gain,   and _____ there   is   love, _____

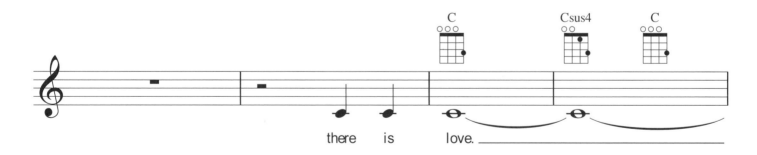

there   is   love. _____

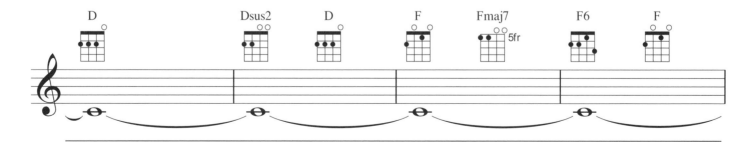

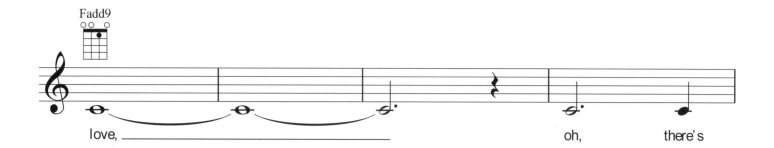

love, _____ oh, there's

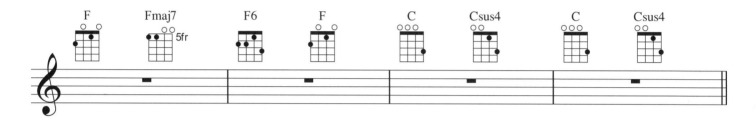

love. _____

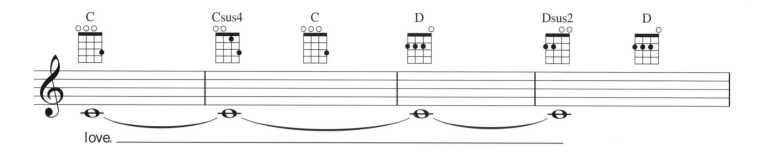

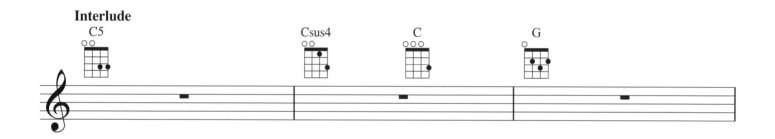

Interlude

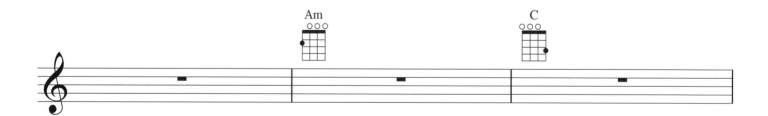

D.S. al Coda

Oh, the

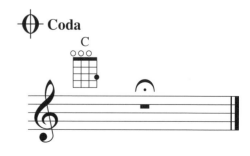

Coda

You Are the Sunshine of My Life

Words and Music by Stevie Wonder

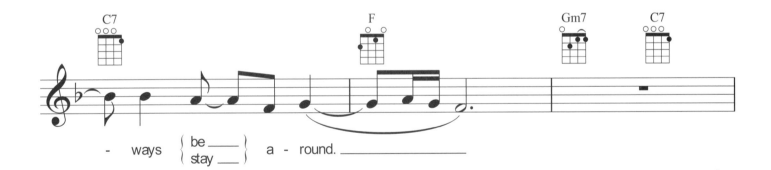

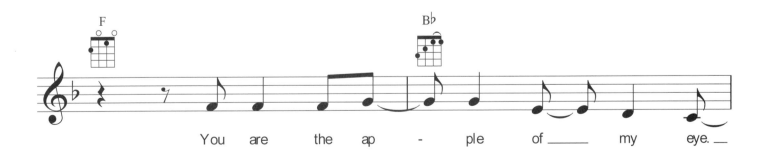

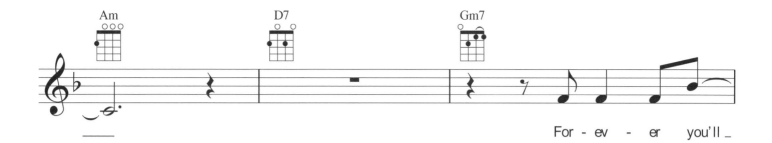

For - ev - er you'll _

To Coda ⊕

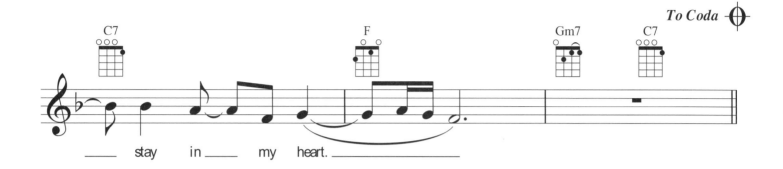

_ stay in _ my heart. _

Verse

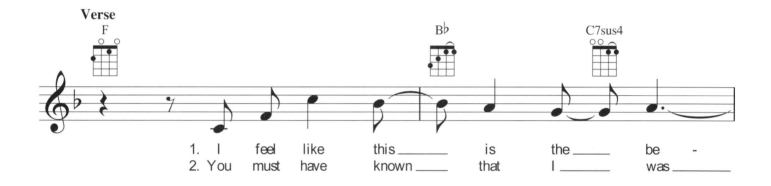

1. I feel like this _____ is the _____ be -
2. You must have known _____ that I _____ was _____

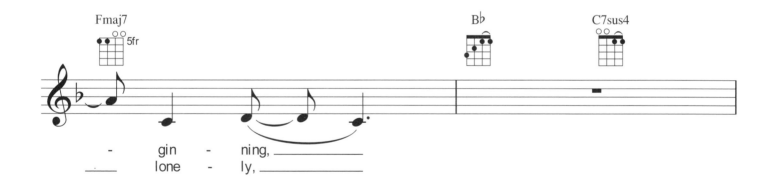

_ - gin - ning, _____
_ lone - ly, _____

'though I've loved you _____ for a mil - lion years. _
be - cause you came _____ to my _____ res - cue. _

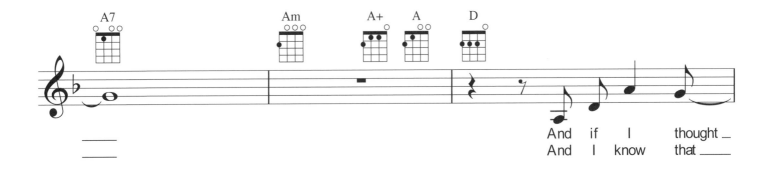

And if I thought ___
And I know that ___

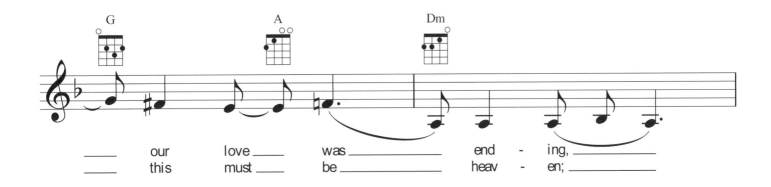

___ our love ___ was ___ end - ing, ___
___ this must ___ be ___ heav - en; ___

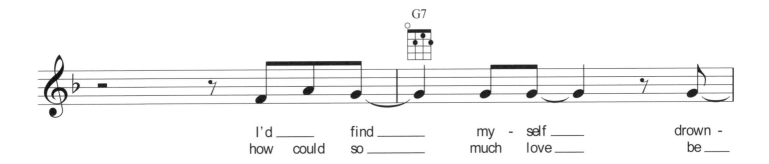

I'd ___ find ___ my - self ___ drown -
how could so ___ much love ___ be ___

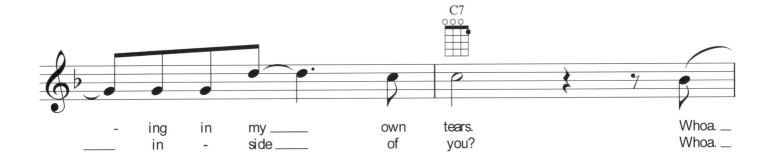

- ing in my ___ own tears.   Whoa. ___
___ in - side ___ of you?   Whoa. ___

2nd time, D.C. al Coda

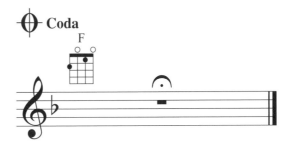

Coda

White Sandy Beach

Words and Music by Willy Dann

1. I saw you in ___ my dream. ___ We were

walk - ing hand ___ in hand ___ on a white ___ sand - y beach ___

___ of Ha - wai - i. ___ 2. We were

play - ing in ___ the sun. ___ We were
(3.) hot, fun sum - mer days ___

hav - ing so ___ much fun ___ }
ly - ing there in the sun ___ } on a white ___

____ sand - y beach ___ of Ha - wai - i. _____

Chorus

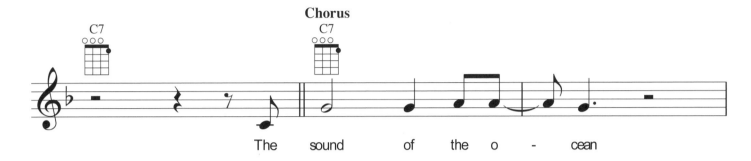

The sound of the o - cean

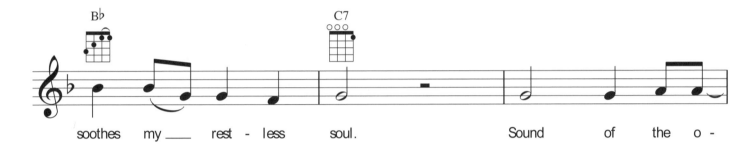

soothes my ___ rest - less soul. Sound of the o -

- cean rocks me all ___ night long. _____

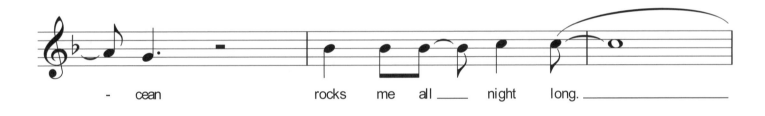

3. Those

Oh, last night ___ in my dreams, ___

I saw your face ___ a - gain. ___ We were there ___

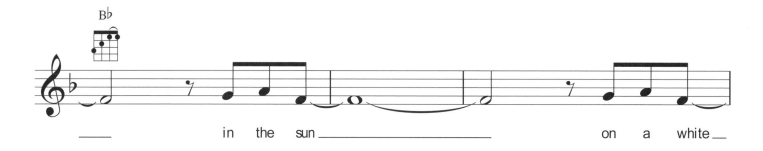

___ in the sun ___ on a white ___

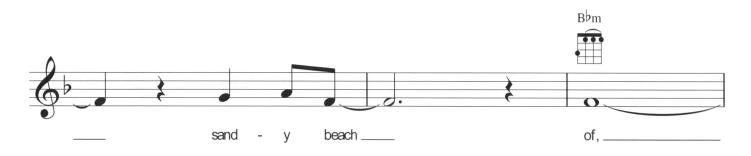

___ sand - y beach ___ of, ___

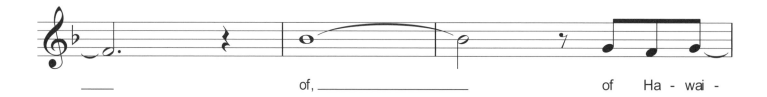

___ of, ___ of Ha - wai -

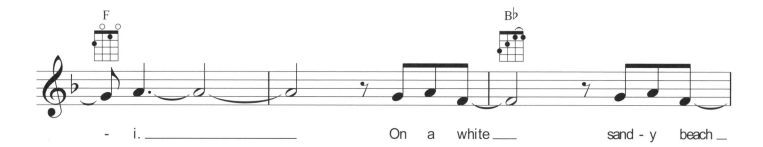

- i. ___ On a white ___ sand - y beach ___

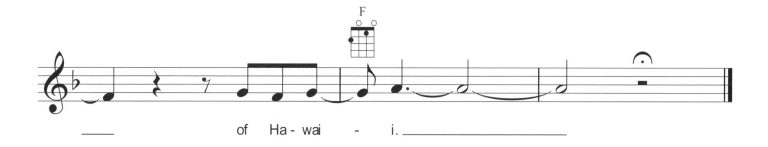

___ of Ha - wai - i. ___

HAL•LEONARD UKULELE PLAY-ALONG®

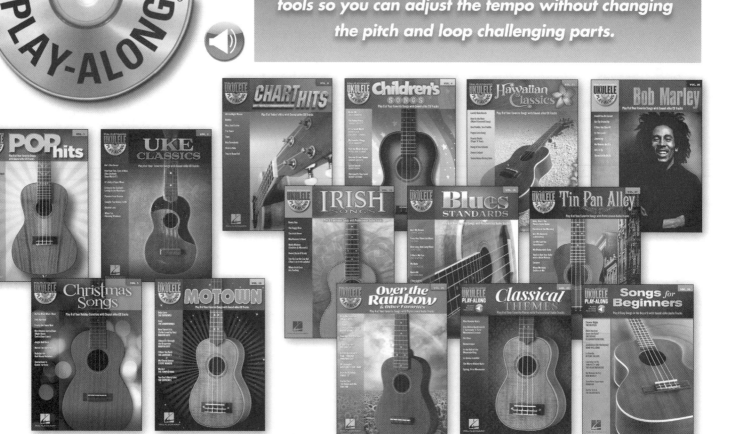

Now you can play your favorite songs on your uke with great-sounding backing tracks to help you sound like a bona fide pro! The audio also features playback tools so you can adjust the tempo without changing the pitch and loop challenging parts.

1. POP HITS
00701451 Book/CD Pack...............$14.99

2. UKE CLASSICS
00701452 Book/CD Pack...............$12.99

3. HAWAIIAN FAVORITES
00701453 Book/CD Pack...............$12.99

4. CHILDREN'S SONGS
00701454 Book/CD Pack...............$12.99

5. CHRISTMAS SONGS
00701696 Book/CD Pack...............$12.99

6. LENNON & MCCARTNEY
00701723 Book/CD Pack...............$12.99

7. DISNEY FAVORITES
00701724 Book/CD Pack...............$12.99

8. CHART HITS
00701745 Book/CD Pack...............$14.99

9. THE SOUND OF MUSIC
00701784 Book/CD Pack...............$12.99

10. MOTOWN
00701964 Book/CD Pack...............$12.99

11. CHRISTMAS STRUMMING
00702458 Book/CD Pack...............$12.99

12. BLUEGRASS FAVORITES
00702584 Book/CD Pack...............$12.99

13. UKULELE SONGS
00702599 Book/CD Pack...............$12.99

14. JOHNNY CASH
00702615 Book/CD Pack...............$14.99

15. COUNTRY CLASSICS
00702834 Book/CD Pack...............$12.99

16. STANDARDS
00702835 Book/CD Pack...............$12.99

17. POP STANDARDS
00702836 Book/CD Pack...............$12.99

18. IRISH SONGS
00703086 Book/CD Pack...............$12.99

19. BLUES STANDARDS
00703087 Book/CD Pack...............$12.99

20. FOLK POP ROCK
00703088 Book/CD Pack...............$12.99

21. HAWAIIAN CLASSICS
00703097 Book/CD Pack...............$12.99

22. ISLAND SONGS
00703098 Book/CD Pack...............$12.99

23. TAYLOR SWIFT
00704106 Book/CD Pack...............$14.99

24. WINTER WONDERLAND
00101871 Book/CD Pack...............$12.99

25. GREEN DAY
00110398 Book/CD Pack...............$14.99

26. BOB MARLEY
00110399 Book/CD Pack...............$14.99

27. TIN PAN ALLEY
00116358 Book/CD Pack...............$12.99

28. STEVIE WONDER
00116736 Book/CD Pack...............$14.99

29. OVER THE RAINBOW & OTHER FAVORITES
00117076 Book/CD Pack...............$14.99

30. ACOUSTIC SONGS
00122336 Book/CD Pack...............$14.99

31. JASON MRAZ
00124166 Book/CD Pack...............$14.99

32. TOP DOWNLOADS
00127507 Book/CD Pack...............$14.99

33. CLASSICAL THEMES
00127892 Book/Online Audio..........$14.99

34. CHRISTMAS HITS
00128602 Book/CD Pack...............$14.99

35. SONGS FOR BEGINNERS
00129009 Book/Online Audio..........$14.99

36. ELVIS PRESLEY HAWAII
00138199 Book/CD Pack...............$14.99

39. GYPSY JAZZ
00146559 Book/Online Audio..........$14.99

HAL•LEONARD® CORPORATION

7777 W. BLUEMOUND RD. P.O. BOX 13819 MILWAUKEE, WI 53213

www.halleonard.com

Prices, contents, and availability subject to change without notice.

0616